WOMEN IN CARS

Winner of the 1992 Marianne Moore Poetry Prize.

The Marianne Moore Poetry Prize was established in 1991 by Helicon Nine, and will be awarded annually to a previously unpublished manuscript selected by a distinguished poet through a nationwide competition.

The judge for 1992 was Colette Inez.

WOMEN IN CARS

Poems

MARTHA MCFERREN

With an Introduction by Colette Inez

HELICON NINE EDITIONS
KANSAS CITY, MISSOURI

Copyright © 1992 by Martha McFerren
Copyright © 1992 by Colette Inez

All rights reserved under International and Pan American Copyright Conventions. Published by Helicon Nine Editions, Kansas City, Missouri. Requests for permission to copy any part of this work should be addressed to the publisher.

The author gratefully acknowledges the editors of the following publications, in which some of these poems previously appeared: *College English, Half Tones to Jubilee, Helicon Nine, Kentucky Poetry Review, Louisiana Literature, New Virginia Review, Plainsong, Poetry Northwest, Poetry Review, Willow Springs, Wormwood Review, Xanadu.*
"Another Martha Graham Routine" appeared as "Contredanse" in *Maple Leaf Rag: An Anthology of New Orleans Poetry* (The New Orleans Poetry Journal Press, 1980).
"Exercise," "Weird Doctors," and "Women in Cars" are reprinted from *Shenandoah: The Washington and Lee University Review*, with the permission of the editor.

The author wishes to express her thanks to the National Endowment for the Arts for a Fellowship in Poetry (1991), which helped her complete this collection.

Cover: Suzan Pitt. *Tamara*, 1986. Acrylic on canvas.
Book design by Tim Barnhart
Printed by Boelte-Hall Litho, Roeland Park, Kansas

Partial funding for this project has been provided by the Kansas Arts Commission and the Missouri Arts Council, state agencies; and by the N. W. Dible Foundation.

This book is printed on recycled, acid-free paper.

Library of Congress Catolog Number: 92-72689

ISBN: 0-9627460-6-1

Manufactured in the United States of America
FIRST EDITION

HELICON NINE EDITIONS • P.O. BOX 22412 • KANSAS CITY MO 64113

My constant thanks to the people who've helped me assemble these poems, particularly Lee Meitzen Grue, Steve Schwartz, Kay Mettelka, Joan Aleshire, Gail Peck, Richard Kilbourne, and Gloria Vando Hickok. Particularly to my mother, who is surviving poetry and who wishes it known the uncle beaten with the buggy whip was an uncle by marriage; the McFerrens may be a bit crazy, but they are not trashy. And to Dennis, who has stayed married for four books. Probably not a record, but it does show good intentions.

An account of Mabel Normand's life is *Mabel*, by Betty Harper Russell. Conflicting versions of the Frankie Silver case can be found in *Cabins in the Laurel*, by Muriel Earley Sheppard and in Manly Wade Wellman's *Dead and Gone*. For more on Miss Ouida Keeton, see Wyatt Cooper's *Families*, specifically the chapter on "Some Dangers of Family Life." The original "Femtype" passage in "Confederate Science Fiction" is of course from the diaries of Mary Boyken Chestnutt; the remainder of Confederate Sci Fi defies explanation if you are not a Southerner with a long memory. And Nim Graves, that wasn't *you* in the poem, but I couldn't resist using your name.

CONTENTS

ix	Introduction by Colette Inez
3	Women in Cars
5	Private Club
6	Southern Gothic
8	Through a Door
10	Train / Time / Train
11	Clouds / Fire / Clouds
12	Puremouth
13	Biographer, Where Are You?
15	Dormitory
17	How To Get Published
19	Die With It in You
21	Mabel Takes a Dive
23	Miss Clay's Establishment
24	Story Lady
25	Exercise
27	Another Martha Graham Routine
29	Confederate Science Fiction
31	First Time Out
34	Tripartite
35	The Baby in the Bath
38	The Power of Television
40	Nim's Big Chill Trip
43	A Moment of Tribute
45	Breakfast Included

46	Sunglasses, 1970; The Rest, 1987
47	Weird Doctors
49	Knees and Necks / New Orleans
51	Pretty Woman
53	The Bad Southern Cooking Poem
55	A Girl Who Loves Her Father
57	Dog Suicide
60	A Metaphor Crosses the Road
61	Cool Places
63	When I Get There
64	Examples

INTRODUCTION

Imagine Holden Caulfield as a woman from New Orleans, and add a dash of a literate Joan Rivers's "can we talk?" gossipy spirit. Then dip back into antebellum days and mix in a feisty Scarlett determined to be noticed. What you will get is something of Martha McFerren's sassy, off-beat, nose-thumbing and altogether original voice. A stand-up comic? Reading McFerren, I broke into laughter more than once—not my usual reaction to poetry manuscripts crossing my desk.

This is not to say she is *all* friskiness and mirth. The quote from her preface: "...Tranquility's a mask. Mask for mask I prefer violence" (Henri-Pierre Roche, *Jules and Jim*), speaks to a dark side—an attraction to the grotesque and the murderous. The grimly dramatic "Die With It in You" showcases the poet's narrative skill:

> Near Toe River in North Carolina, 1831,
> Charlie Silver was dozing by the fireplace.
> Frankie Silver lifted their baby Nancy
> out of his arms and divorced him with an ax.

and the chill of "Cool Places" haunts the reader with its incisive truth of family life:

> ...thin lips
> built our smiles, thin loves our marriages
> which endured through glaciers.
> We've become soul-scoured, hunkering
> on panoramic grudges, and take our cures
> in a soul-scouring wind.

But if macabre ballads and stoical forays into fields of buried pain show McFerren's emotional range, it is the verve and effervescence of the language, and a keenly-developed sense of the absurd that endear the reader to her world. And the world she gives us in generous portions is Southern—deep-South Louisiana with a nod to East Texas. Scenes of "Mama and her meat and the pie with flies" offer up the butterbeans and okra of bad Southern cooking which McFerren deliciously satirizes, along with the "lush disease known as Southern Gothic."

The poet's sense of place transcends mere landscaping, suggested by the names she casts for her motley characters, mad Ouida Keeton and genteel Miss Rachel Parrish married to the "loud evangelist," Mercer Gale Pitts, and Everette, fearless Teddie Sue, and the happy and hapless

Nim Graves who is discovered making love on frozen ground. McFerren's Louisiana, bereft of dreamy bayous and balustrades, is also a state where an aging couple seeking to leap into oblivion is hard put to find a cliff.

   A Southern allegiance to family and friends, and a harking back to the past informs these poems: among them the wacky and madcap "Confederate Science Fiction" in which inimitable extraterrestrials address Jefferson Davis. With another sidelong glance at Memory Lane, Southern-style, the poet pokes fun at the new commercialism in "Breakfast Included":

> Old towns are business: the light
> gets reinvigorated, spritzed with sugar
> for that syrupy, translucent glister:
> you walk through grapefruit cordial.
> Libraries: white and filled with diaries . . .

Mostly, her ramble through time pulls us back into nineteen-sixties' popular culture: innocent sex, TV's *Medical Center*, Eugene McCarthy's entry into politics (to have his poems read we are told), days curled up with *Atlas Shrugged* and *The Feminine Mystique*, college life whose pathos is leavened with hilarity.

   It is a spiky and self-assured voice we hear in these flashbacks; her ear for speech is as sharp as Teddie Sue's verbal assault on an amorous young man in a car's front seat:

> Get your hands off me,
> you barbarian, you homosapiens,
> you despicable, blue-balled
> lower primate. . .
>   ("The Baby in the Bath")

"Mabel Takes a Dive" written from the point of view of Mabel Normand, of silent movies, sends out similar sparks:

> Kick me and I'll kick you back.
> I'll shove a creampuff in your puss
> and some firecrackers in your britches . . .

   In "How To Get Published" McFerren uses the same scrappy voice for pot shots at the literary establishment while describing the ordeals poets endure. She won my belly-laugh when spinning out the wistful portrait of a seeker after literary fame:

> Into the night she hurries,
> book in hand, the dogs of simile
> behind her yelping *Like! Like! Like!*

Women in Cars is an exhilarating collection that invites us on high-speed and sometimes wonderfully reckless journeys. McFerren turns up the music or plays it cool, and we catch an earful of her comic sorcery as she comes to terms with mid-life, a time and place where only Raquel Welch's "spirits, breasts and hemlines never fell."

The poet writes in "Biographer, Where Are You?": "It is better to be the magician than magicked . . . Fata Morgana is a pretty good job description." In that bewitching post Martha McFerren already has tenure.

— Colette Inez
Judge
9 May 1992

When Lucie had gone, Kate said, "Tranquility's a mask. Mask for mask, I prefer violence."
—Henri-Pierre Roche, *Jules and Jim*

Judy shivered. It reminded her of more than one past adventure—the seven clues she had found in her own cellar, a terrifying night locked in with the Chinaman's spooks and the mysterious shadow she had seen in the cellar of a little house on upper Grove Street.
—Margaret Sutton, *The Midnight Visitor*

Your present will be determined by your past. Therefore in the future you should be very careful what you do in your past!
—"Ziggy" cartoon

Be careful—the inevitable might happen.
—My mother

WOMEN IN CARS

More women have done this
than you'd imagine.

You're out there driving
back from Grand Saline or wherever
they made something happen
that particular Saturday.
Actually *he's* doing the driving
and you're just sitting there
twiddling with the radio.

It's night on a two-lane blacktop.
There's nobody in the state,
except the stuff that's
been run over, and
already your date is yelling,
"Let's play like we're
in England," and scooting over
to the opposite lane
every ten minutes or so,
and you are so awfully bored.

So you start taking off
your clothes, starting with
your shoes, then your earrings,
then your shirt and bra.
Getting out of your
blue jeans isn't easy.
You have to hoist your rump
and buck forward with your knees
like you're doing the limbo,
but let's admit it,
climbing out of jeans in cars
is a native art.

When I was driving
with a boy named Frank Fallis,
I even whipped off my phony
ponytail and threw it

in the back seat, and he screamed,
"GAAAAAA," and skidded off
the road. And then he said,
really sarcastic, "You got
anything *else* unnatural?"

You can ride hours like that
with the wind and the bugs
blowing all over you,
and some Wilson Pickett.
If you go through a place
like Scofield or La Tuna
you don't even need to duck.
They're all in bed
with their shades down,
dreaming about rain.

There's simply nothing out there.
Some people say Texans
think more about wheels than sex,
but you have to understand
the distances involved.

PRIVATE CLUB

It's as easy as breathing; it *is* breathing.
You don't just cruise Dairy Queens,
crunching ice and talking to the girls
who travel in trios and quartets,
daddy's car keys in hand, their hair
up in curlers for somebody nicer.
You don't just drive the farm roads.
Go out there in the dark, you're not
plugging stop signs, tossing cherry bombs.

Girl at a slumber party, not asleep,
nose to a shut screen door, flirting with
the tenth boy come to say hello.
"Been out driving?" she asks.
Out that crazy way, on your own.
"Been frog sticking." But no frog,
not even a Texas frog, took the skin off
his knuckles, put that raw flush on him.

Kid in a bar, just old enough to be there,
smashing his fist down, saying, "I am
Herman Edd Heinz, and I can slice your ass
fifty-seven ways." Lug wrenches. Knives.

The one thing girls won't do, can't do—
not like this. Jimmy and me in a roadhouse
by the county line, just wanting hamburgers.
Over a secret door arc red neon palm trees,
orange neon letters: PRIVATE CLUB.
What do they do back there?
He shuts both eyes, one fist, thumb over
hard. "They fight," Jimmy whispers.

SOUTHERN GOTHIC

for Everette Maddox and Eugene Walter

Poet in New York, revised. "Where you from?"
asks the woman in the Horn and Hardart
of the man with a tie wider than he is.
"Alabama," he answers. She's uncorked.

From her green beans she rises. "When,"
she yells in compassion, "will you SLIME
stop murdering Negroes?" and this frail man,
who only did damage to himself
with too much Scotch, hunkers down
in a city of razor wire, not thinking
to holler in return, "When will you YANKEES
stop mugging the Hasidim for their diamonds?"

You don't need this, Everette.
Come home, listen to your own folks
make idiots of themselves. And come back,
Eugene, from Rome, where the Communists
beat you up. Come home and let your own folks
work you over at Mardi Gras.

                               And go home, me,
where it's a mess, but a warmer, cheaper one.
Where nobody stares at my flat noises,
nobody stands on good geography
waiting, wide-white-eyed, for me to swig
a jar of moonshine and go South blind,
to kick a hound dog, whip out the whip.
They're sure I carry it, that lush disease
known as Gothic.

                 I should tell them,
That's man stuff, anyway. We womenfolk,
we only sat saying things. Like the woman
at the asylum, slamming down her hand
and shouting, "I will not play another card,

Ouida Keeton, until you tell me
what you did with the rest of your mother!"

Okay, so Miss Ouida, *she* took some action,
but usually we talk.

"They sewed
that tube to her BLADDER, and all the curl
fell out of her hair. Never did come back
'cept for one little patch."
"She had
a heart attack and laid there
three days next to the clothesline
with her face in the clematis
and the ANTS ate her."

Miss Mae Marie
asked the cop with the ice cream,
"You all find out 'bout them two men
that was hangin' in the TREE?"
Oh, not the Klan this time, just a suicide
with company.

The only person I know
who ever got whipped was my Uncle Jesse,
because, in 1910, he left off plowing
and slipped away to the schoolhouse.
His father tied him around a tree, beat him
ignorant with a buggy whip.
They do it to
kids up North, too. They just do it indoors.

THROUGH A DOOR

The door itself
makes no promises.
It is only a door.
— Adrienne Rich

It was evening, we were cold,
we covered that round magic
in seventy-four locomotive minutes.

My friend Joe Bruchac
came here to the stones
with his eagle bone whistle
and blew it to four directions.
But, damn, we weren't up to that.
It's hard getting through
two bloody millennia per week.
No Stonehenge, no way.
And now, only one late hour
for the whole of Avebury: pictures,
tea in the pub, buying earrings.

But up on the ancient bank
where we dodged some herefords,
I saw the enormous crimson sun
going plop between two sarsens:
fifty tons, each of them,
and flat as the ten commandments.

"The wide ones are women,"
said our cabby, the authority,
"and the high ones are blokes."
"You'd never prove it," I said,
wanting hard facts or nothing.

Only two dawns later
on the red eye express for London,
I saw that sun come rising
exactly between the towers,
cooling towers, I guess they were,

of a spanking nuclear plant,
the two of them slammed there
like giant unbalanced diabolos.

They were very high.
Probably both blokes.

TRAIN / TIME / TRAIN

Even now we want trains
to be heaven or hell on wheels.
When I was a little kid
I could hear a train
coming like a witness
in the late summer night,
through the blackberries
and crickets and bobwire fences
and through fifty years itself,
though no trains ran
within a decade of our house.
This was in Texas,
which is like no place else.
My mother decided,
Sound travels farther
here in the country.
But I knew it was a ghost.

CLOUDS / FIRE / CLOUDS

I used to dream of Heaven
and wake up screaming
late Sunday nights.

I didn't like those
flat treeless clouds
or Jesus sitting there
in his Jesus tableau
with bunches of little kids,
some of them in turbans.

I wanted to stay down here.
I wasn't sure I liked it
but I was used to it—
dogs, grassburrs,
the whole solid mess.

My parents came running in
from *What's My Line?*

You don't have to go,
they told me. My father
brought me apple juice.
Nobody has to go
if she doesn't want to.
I was only five.
They knew soon enough
I'd hear about the fire.

PUREMOUTH

The puremouth woman comes into my bedroom
in nubby-fibered slacks, her hair blunt-bobbed.
She tears the electric blanket
from my pajamas, screaming, "Microwave!
Microwave!" crushing the cord with her heel;
it's a serpent with a plug. Electricity
drools from cracked sockets. My cabinet
has pills, my fillings are chock with mercury.
If I were awake, I wouldn't put up with this.

She's turning my pictures to the walls,
my prints and watercolors; the cardboard
used for matting has eventually lethal rays.
"Aren't you concerned for the children?"
What children? She shows me two children,
both girls, both of them naked, since
fabric retards growth. The two little girls
have a ho-hum attitude, look awfully healthy.
Hold it, these kids don't live here,
why can't my art irradiate?
I have no children, can't. I color my hair.
I have dyed my brain Flame, my blood is full of
substitute red. *I knew this. I did it anyway.*
The puremouth roots through magazines.
If I lick the pages, she informs me,
the ink is poisonous. At the least I
should ship them to prisons; whatever happens
is an advantage. She scrubs my toilet.

The two bored girls are looking peckish.
Though I don't know much about children,
I know what they like. "Kids, want a cookie?"
The puremouth starts blotching—
Daffy Duck inflating into a bagpipe.
"Food?!" she's screaming, "FOOD?!...."

BIOGRAPHER, WHERE ARE YOU?

Martha McFerren, having worn
caftan-and-heavy-earring, then
tweed-and-glasses, progressed to black,
dire, slimming, alienated black,
and hauled her turquoise out again.
She went to graduate school
and learned that every second woman
wore black to think. Nevertheless,
she continued wearing it,
since it hid all the stains.
She started reading books with
"synthesis," "revisionist"
or "prehistoric" in the title.
Her husband said, "It's time you gave up
DANCE and GREEN, sweetie."
She said, "I'll give up DANCE and GREEN
if you stop using PALAVER, HOWL,
FLUMMOX and DISCOMBOBULATE, you
repetitious bastard. Men are
divorced for less." She found out
getting published is an awful lot
like not getting published,
and noticed she'd kept the poems
written to her, including the one
that said she had brown eyes
and the one titled "DOOM DOOM DOOM"
and left unsigned. She tried a
con job, Poetry in the Schools,
where she got called obscene
without even trying for a change.
One boy wrote, "I want to be God."
She said she understood. A girl
announced, "I want to be Mrs. God."
Miss Martha told her
it is better to be the magician
than the magicked. Fata Morgana
is a pretty good job description.

She was going to buy a lipstick
to write big red words
on the principal's forehead, but
the grant ran out. She packed her
GREEN and DANCE, quit being Miss Martha
and went to do something else.

DORMITORY

That Friday I got stood up,
I was on the dormitory steps
waiting for Devlin Tolbert
and his big black motorcycle.
They never got there.
And though I enjoyed the change,
I did catch up with him
next Monday in English 102
and I asked politely
where the hell he'd been.
Well, he'd been coming, honest,
but he'd made a wrong turn
on the Nine Mile Road and thought
he might as well keep going
to Corpus Christi, only
another four hours. And he had
a superior weekend, thanks,
and would I like a froggie
made out of seashells?

But Devlin was okay, really,
if you didn't send him for your
dry cleaning and expect to get it.
I heard how Judy Plante
chased Devlin with a butcher knife
through the Spring Branch Cemetery
at 10:15 one Thursday night.
Midnight is better for stuff
like that, but all us girls
had curfew at eleven, weeknights,
and I'll bet it was hard enough
to get Devlin, the cemetery,
and the butcher knife together
all at once. I don't know why
she picked on Devlin, since she
hardly knew the little bastard.
Maybe she liked his name.

Devlin was saying he didn't mind,
anything's fun the first time.
Or at least interesting.
Maybe he meant it, because he never
turned Judy in, assuming he knew
what he ought to turn her in for.
Anyway, that was our business.
We knew the rules. The girls
had to come in by eleven
and be locked up, and the boys
had to not get killed.

That's easy enough. And Judy
wouldn't have been expelled
if she hadn't killed a rooster
in the dorm and drained its blood
and hung it out her window
on a scarlet cord. Mrs. Kelly
hauled her to Dean Richardson,
the one who kept telling us
she was there for us, but her
teeth looked tight. They said
it was witchcraft, but Judy said
she was *not* a witch. She was a
vampire and damned proud of it.
So they expelled her, and she
joined the WACs. She shouldn't
have pushed it, because it's
great, being an undergraduate.
You don't have to study, even,

at the right really bad college.

HOW TO GET PUBLISHED

*Eugene McCarthy ran for President
to get his poetry published.*
—Lee Meitzen Grue

This wouldn't have happened
if she'd gone to Iowa.
She'd have been on her second volume now:
hitting up Bread Loaf
for a Fellowship,
keeping cracker-crisp records
of verse submitted.

She'd have sat in cafes with wooden tables,
drinking Pernod, dancing
with men in sweaters,
men who whispered lush cream vellum
and limited editions.

Now a samba in the distance:
nonverbal alternative.
"Yes," she imagines, fumbling her tweezers,
"Yes, if I'd gone to Iowa
I wouldn't be here now,
threatened and unpublished
longing for rescue
the way poets long for mail."

How can we tell the dancer from the dance?
and the microdot fits neatly
under a curlicue of query.
Darn good question, Mr. Yeats.
And she closes the book.
Danger. Perspiration.
Why hadn't she hooked herself a doctor
and started her own small press?
Why isn't she in Iowa?

Into the night she hurries,
book in hand, the dogs of simile

behind her yelping *Like! Like! Like!*
through Carnival-drenched streets,
obnoxious Latins spitting on her pumps
when she says, "Move it, buster!"
Samba, samba. Putrid mangoes.

Who's the masked Harlequin?
Quickly—an adjective denoting
both terror and sexual ambition!
"I'll be a cult," she realizes,
approaching the coming knife.
Knife! Think! Exactly what kind of knife?

Erased in Rio on the jacket,
hard covers, and her old prof as executor,
the works! The holy works at a last!
"Raped by a sliver of experience!"
she ventures at a gasp,
dying forward
into next year's criticism.

DIE WITH IT IN YOU

Near Toe River in North Carolina, 1831,
Charlie Silver was dozing by the fireplace.
Frankie Silver lifted their baby Nancy
out of his arms and divorced him with an ax.
He'd flirted some at barn raisings,
in particular with a Mrs. Cranberry
whom Frankie mistrusted, and over there
that's plenty. "Tetchy," they call it.

An apprentice conjurer volunteered.
Over a map, he dangled a red glass ball.
"The body ain't gone North or South or East . . .
or West." "It's got to have gone somewhere,"
said Charlie's father. The next consultant,
skinny old Jakie Collis, whang-leather Holmes
and miraculous tracker, entered the cabin,
took a sniff around and said, "The ashes
is too greasy." He combed the fireplace,
collecting fragments of bone and buckle,
and teeth like over-flung dice.
                                    The widow
had scoured the floorboards, not the dirt
under the floorboards. There in the earth
and on the arcs of puncheon, Jakie Collis
found lots of young blood. Another hound,
the four-legged sort, snuffled Charlie's guts
(which were maybe asbestos) in a hollow tree.
She should have made soap from the ashes
and sausages of his innards. Her relatives,
because you've got to do it, tried hiding her
but they were grabbed.
                                    She mounted the gallows
eating gingerbread, and the hangman asked,
"Frances Silver, are you ready to depart?"
"Gotta finish my cake," she told him,
and after that last sweet swallow, Frankie
opened her mouth to declaim. The crowd below

went still and deliberate, hoping this woman might actually talk some sense; but her father yelled, "Die with it in you, Frankie!"

. . . And damned if she didn't.

MABEL TAKES A DIVE

> *We used to go into a park with a stepladder, a bucket of whitewash and Mabel Normand and make a picture.*
> — Charlie Chaplin

Kick me and I'll kick you back.
I'll shove a creampuff in your puss
and some firecrackers in your britches.
I can handle myself, Mr. Pieface.
Old Griffith's girlies,
those blah little ghosts in pancake,
they never thought of it. So easy:
just kick me and I'll kick you back.

Sound is too much work.
They keep saying, "Slow down, kid.
Go home and learn your lines."
Fat chance. If I wanted conversation
I'd have stayed in New York.
Out here you bounce some oranges.
You see how fast you can go.

Look, I do my own stunts—
goats, marching bands, everything.
I think I even got killed
a couple of times. When Fatty
was paddling his bed downstream,
you think I wasn't drowning, too,
in my own little bed? I mean,
it can get dangerous
in the old fast frame.

And somebody's sainted mother
with a rutched neck keeps braying,
"Shun the laughing girl, my precious.
A laughing girl will lead you
to destruction, to restaurants!"
I ask you—why shouldn't a girl

have a laugh or two?

Bob that little Nellie pigtail
and rubes past Albany start yelling
you're a wicked city woman.
Got a stuffed Pekinese on your sofa.
Any chump who kisses you
will catch the Chinese Gongo
so his slapstick turns blue
and drops right off. Sweet Jesus,
and they believe that malarkey!

You can have a dozen sugar cookies
swooning and whimpering
and getting themselves done to
on that bad old silver flicker
with acres of phony backlot corn,
but it's over. It is really over.
Nobody's going back to the farm.

I was always news at the beach
in my pink Kellermans
and a cute bandanna.
In this business, any stunt
is a genuine spectacular.
Mack had his megaphone
he was waving like a wing of Gabriel.
He yelled, "Jump, baby, jump!"
And I threw out my arms, and I
dove off the edge of the world.

MISS CLAY'S ESTABLISHMENT

That final year, Miss Clay's red album
held a strange diminution of pupils.
Pages of ovals where their faces
would have lain in halftone were empty
but for five or six, all labeled "married to—"
in delectable copperplate. The others
were never mentioned, not even by
visible graduates, who turned the subject
quickly to shortbread and testaments.

Years later Mrs. Japeth Brown,
née Miss Rachel Parrish, one of the missing,
was discovered indoors in Louisville,
increasingly quiet, and married
to a loud evangelist. Though hesitant,
she spoke of her first hungry night,
how she and Miss Ellen Shaw of Rosedown
went looking for roast beef in the pantry
and discovered—(Here Mrs. Brown withdrew,
requesting several small brandies.)

Say you heard a flying skirt, or noticed
red lines in the needlepoint, or felt a paw. . .
They've said the devil is a fiddler,
a lawyer, or a civil servant. I have learned
the devil is a chaperone, inspecting ears,
dropping something depressing in the soup.
How intriguing if, after such commitment,
the gentlemen were deceived.
The school was reopened. New management.

STORY LADY

"Assume they know nothing," says Mrs. Nye.
Black herself, she says it fearlessly.
"Not Cinderella, not left from right
or how to peel a banana. One little boy
doesn't know his name. Just call him Boo."

But what the hell. All little kids—
white, black or burnt sienna—want to know
less nothing. I don't know diddly myself;
I wear sane shoes and keep my eyes open,
and that's about it. Except for stories.

Stories with pictures. Pictures count.
Sometimes, even now, when I close my eyes
I get the metamorphosis. Me the girl;
my Wicked StepQueen and those seven
times a dozen illustrated dwarfs.

Splits of myself, a woman told me.
Very unwicked, but crazy with I Ching
and thin in a caftan. She took my wrist
and whispered, "Trust your little men.
Your little men and multiples of four
will save you." But let's skip that.

What's bad is opening the book,
no matter which dwarfs, and showing them
those separate bricks of print,
each four-cornered and chock with
the same old safety. How do you start on,
"This is major stuff, kids! ALPHABET. . ."?
How can you even say, "Your little men
will save you"? When on every page
you also have to say, "Snow White. . .
Snow White. . ."?

EXERCISE

for Dennis

He's having the mid-life crisis
he promised me he wouldn't have.
"You only crash," he explained,
"if you haven't reached your dreams.
But I've never known what I wanted."
He knows now what he wants: *young*.

He looks in the long mirror,
tugging the slack in his jacket,
looks in his shaving mirror,
even with no razor, examines
the new jowling, the graying,
the thickening around the bend.
He's mumbling about fifty,
though he's three years from fifty.
He likes to brood ahead.

At least I know where he is:
in the basement pumping iron.
He hasn't emptied the bank account
and split for India to find himself
amidst the rice. In cold light
I check him out and decide,
He still looks mighty good.
He deserves a straw boater
and spiffy white cricket flannels,
cricket flannels let out a trifle.
Women pay boodles in beauty parlors
for that silver in the forelock.

I haven't done panic yet. I was
old before my time; the time
just seems to be catching up.
McFerrens age well. We're crazy,
but we keep our hair and our hides.
Still, it's coming. The two of us
have discussed holding hands

when it gets too awful, and jumping
off the first cliff we can find,
which would take some driving
in Louisiana. I suggested handcuffs,
in case one pulls a cop-out
and stands there yelling, "SOR-ry,"
while the other heads for the dirt.

I don't lift weights, but mornings
after he's left for work,
I put on my 45's and dance. Fast.

ANOTHER MARTHA GRAHAM ROUTINE

In their hearts
they never left the stormy coast;
each night on the flatbed prairie
the father assembles his children
and reads from the classics,
then extinguishes the flame
in its shallow basin.
He sets up tragedy
like another barn.

On that playbill of degenerates
an ambitious farm hand
decides he wants the daughter,
and in that very house
resplendent with store-bought tassels.
In he slides
just after quiet
for an angular grapple
under her red quilt.

They sleep an hour afterward;
then in comes her brother
with a crescent knife.
Before she wakens
he carves up her lover
and leaves for Texas.

When she sits up
she doesn't scream
at this great bulk of silence,
doesn't rub his blood
across her superficial breasts.
She's been waiting
in this cotton gown
for the certain release
of a disaster.

She will not die.
Over her thin carpet

she dances
to the music of cold rooms,
could never dance
without the family
in a watching semicircle,
staring black volumes
at her sure fall and recovery.

She could never dance
without the family
and their acres
of devotions and potatoes
and rich alfalfa,
without the curse
of an old man
back in New Hampshire.
But dance she does, superbly,
in a landscape
as wide as what she hates.

CONFEDERATE SCIENCE FICTION

A spaceship lands. Two frogfaces
named Ol'Bleu and Grae climb out,
both of them chartreuse. They approach

President Jefferson Davis, who is
sitting reading *Guy Mannering* by lamplight.
Grae speaks: "Mistah Davis, suh,

don't you let that no-good General Hood
assume command in Jawjah.
'Cause if he does—yawl gonna FALL."
Great silence from President Jeff.
"That's accordin' to Bruce Catton, suh.
Code name: Daddy Warbooks."

                                            Mistah Davis
reaches for the brandy decanter,
imbibes several megacolossal swallows.

Thin air,
            and in the thin air voices:
"Ours is a monstrous system. Any Femtype
can tell you the progenitor
of satellites by her neighbor's planet.
Those near her own, she thinks,
warped from Sector 8."
                            "Let us cross Orion
and rest beneath the Horsehead Nebula."
"Chat Ta Nooga."
                        Despite frog warning,
Jeff makes him some mule noggin moves.
                            South loses,

yet voices continue: "Forty acres
and a zwoot." "Chick A Mog." "Ga Kreek."
"Oooooh, you bad old Thang,
why did you nuke my papa's cotton?"
"Mars Rob Ert."
                            "We got us a cane bomb,

got us a ready and able bomb. I DO BELIEVE
the Yawp is gonna rise—"
                        MOREOVER,
when Jud Smith charged at Malvern Hill
he kept going into the fire and was
never seen or heard of again. Then
his old daddy charged at Iuka likewise,
and he, too, was NEVER SEEN OR
HEARD OF AGAIN
                    . . . .*aliens*.

FIRST TIME OUT

It was always the same:
Saturdays, midnight,
the elevators opening,
this boozed-up cube of girls
hitting pocked linoleum.

Five floors of it,
five hundred Freshmen
who were not men,
some in big fits
because they'd gotten laid,
Anne Clancy hysterical
because she hadn't been,
again. "He wouldn't do it,"
she'd be sobbing, the
de-virgination
postponed another week
by her one scared sweetie,
"he wouldn't dooooo iiiiit!"

Stephanie Musselwhite
always fell out in sections
like a badly propped phonebook.
She'd have a silk cravat
around her throat
to make her look sophisticated
and hide her hickeys.
But what she looked like
was Samuel Taylor Coleridge;
plus she'd strangle
when she was vomiting
and I'd have to jiggle her
by her fat brown bangs.
By November she'd left.

By December half were gone.
They got caught sneaking out—
or in—or blowing a bit of
Mexican boo smoke.

They flunked on purpose
and told their parents, "See?
Now can I marry Donnie?"
Others just plain eloped.
And some, bless their hearts,
flunked by accident
from playing jacks all night.

They missed the city.
Old friends. Television.
A couple swore
they missed their mothers.
A few would not eat
what was on those trays,
not even the apricot pie.
Sometimes their fathers
just came and got them.

This world of parents
actually had the gall
to act surprised.
It was time to get running,
time to start being the opposite
of whatever we'd had to be
at seventeen.

Elaine Von Haselberg
had the first go-go boots,
white, with just enough scuff,
and she kept saying, "Call me
Eldorique—that's Q-U-E."
But then she had to go and
get herself pregnant
by an embarrassment—
not only a Mercer Pitts
but a Mercer Gale Pitts!

Before Elaine went home
she came and told me

she'd wanted to be like me.
"Because," she said,
"you know what you truly want."
By this she meant I
had a boy picked out
and he was not desperate,
which to us seemed
great raving maturity.
She believed in me
and I did, too, but
when it all came apart,
that was the biggest joke.

TRIPARTITE

When Chris was drafted
Jennie got his apartment
and I'd go visit her
and we'd talk things over.
I knew she was thinking,
"He won't marry Martha,
he'll marry me."
And I was thinking,
"He may not marry me
but he'll never marry her."

In our separate faiths
we got along nicely.
She even showed me
how she'd glued his photo
in the bottom of the toilet.
I mean, she wanted
to marry the man,
but she knew what he was.
I never guessed
she was already pregnant.

Of course I was right.
Chris didn't marry
either one of us.
Actually, it's more like
we didn't marry him.
Years later at some party
we met the woman
he'd finally married,
and we fled to the kitchen
and laughed like bitches.

THE BABY IN THE BATH

For a girl who loved animals
she sure liked cutting them up.
I found her elbow-deep in shark
when I wandered into biology
to borrow her history notes,
and she was grinning
at that gash with teeth
in a sort of sawboned empathy.

I suppose she did love animals.
We loved pronouncing them:
slow loris, dikdik, tufted titmouse.
She could say *marsupial*
with a persimmony hiss and pucker.

One Saturday night her bathtub
had a marsupial in it.
A possum, to be exact,
dumped where he couldn't escape,
only pitter his little claws
against the porcelain.
How she got him past Grendel's Mother,
our very *loco parentis*, I don't know.
She'd stolen him.

Not for good, of course.
She was going to put him back
and do the formaldehyde number,
but she wanted me to look.

Have you ever seen a possum prick?
It's pronged! Like a messed-up trident
or a quick scholastic bracket.
Possumprick.
We said it several times.

Next time it was a baby.
"My god, Teddie Sue!" I yelled,
"where did you get the kid?"

"Shut up!" she said.
"That girl at the Pizza Inn
is getting married,
so I told her I'd hold Whatsit."

What did we know about babies?
Our mothers hadn't done it since us.
Another little specimen,
tappety tapping small-scale nails
against the off-white grunge
and gumming a bunnyrabbit.
We managed, the pair of us,
to rotate his diapers.

She couldn't dissect him
like the shark or the marsupial:
he didn't belong to her.
But frankly, I did not trust
her incisive little eyes.

Why is it people talk about
girls going wild
and they mean only one thing,
when a girl can flip her flapjacks
in every way except that?
Teddie Sue was the all-around
most dangerous virgin
you ever poked a stick at.

She'd get a boy in a car somewhere
and let his hand get
right to the water margin.
Then she'd start thumping him
and shrieking, "Get your hands off me,
you barbarian, you homosapiens,
you despicable blue-balled
lower primate! DARWIN WOULD WEEP!"
She had a great left knee,
a nail file, and an instinct

for picking nice guys and dorks.

An immaculate instinct.
She could handle anything with ears.
No pills, no diaphragm,
no just-in-case. Never her.
The rest of us were sluts.

There was this guy named Leon.
Guess how long it took.

I did come in and sit
and read to her from *Atlas Shrugged*
most of one Saturday
while she boiled in the tub
trying to start a flow.
They tell you that old wives' trick
doesn't work. This time it did.

Well, something did.

THE POWER OF TELEVISION

I think it was *Medical Center*.
You know, one of those shows
where they cure you quick
and still have time to hustle Pontiacs.
This girl had gone to college
and fallen off a ladder
and needed a kidney. Carrie Snodgress
was the girl, the same Carrie Snodgress
who, years later,
was in the sack with some actor
when a record mogul named Nitzsche
came home and caught them
and expressed his unhappiness
by shoving a pistol up the
pertinent section of Carrie's anatomy.
Nitzsche got charged with "rape
by instrumentality," a new one on me,
and said, "I still feel friendly
toward her."
                    Pat Hingle
was Carrie's father. He was a yeller.
Fathers yell if their daughters
are majoring in Commie pinko atheist
with a graduate degree
in Whore of Babylon. Of course
he gave her a kidney. I was there
in the big red chair, in from college,
watching Pat Hingle
in a wheelchair next to Carrie's bed.
"Honey," he said, "I love you,
I really do. Just couldn't say it."
Tears on his cheeks. "I never was
any good at this stuff."
                            My father
looked toward the bathroom.
He said, "That goes for me, too,
kid," his eyes on the bathtub

I should have cleaned. I looked
into the kitchen. I have to tell you
I have faith in television.
It helps you communicate
and nobody has to lose a kidney.
Those people who shouldn't talk,
they can still be together
and their mouths needn't move
except for the beer and popcorn.
When families talk, sometimes
they shoot each other. Watch TV.

NIM'S BIG CHILL TRIP

He quit his job
teaching computation theory
and drove through eleven states
saying hi there
wherever he could find us,
seeing what was up.

We'd never been lovers,
so we hadn't done much to each other.
We hadn't done much at all,
only been together
in the same dumb places.

Good old Nim.
The same Nim Graves
I'd been in messes with.
Except his eyebrows
had gotten gray and gnarly,
like electrocuted moss.
"Wow," I thought, "has he got eyebrows!"
And a second later, a second lower,
"Wow, has he got eyes!"
Still pale. That same old ice.

Like at the Archie party.

We called it an Archie party
because of old Archie
in his sweat-stained hat—
even then, in January—
with his sharecropper's guitar
and rusty harmonica,
getting hyped by us
in the usual student dump.

I was right there, eighteen
and planning to get some life,
though I was not crazy, like Jilly
who passed out a virgin

and woke up pregnant.
I was easing in gradually:
my first hard liquor,
my first non-white brassiere,
the first time I'd say "piss."

I stood there with a glass.
Archie was singing
"My Baby Done Changed
the Lock on the Door."
Nim was outside throwing up,
and the heater was making smoke.

I went to check on Nim
outside the shack
and found him under it,
stretched out with Michelle
on the frozen crust of mud
that made a rectangle,
the two of them cold stone naked.
In a sort of crescendo
they'd even removed their socks.

There they rose, their torsos
blue-whitely radiant
and intertwined—
static, in fact, at
some obtuse, unbelievable pitch.
Two clear phoenixes
who were going to catch pneumonia.

I only looked a minute,
out of pure journalism.
You really have to consider
if you're up for
that sort of fucking on thin ice
with no Trojans or blankets.
Maybe not wanting any,
maybe not even thinking about it.

That's always my problem,
thinking about it.

When I got inside
Jimmy asked me, "Is Nim okay?"
"Sure," I said
and drank the glass of water
somebody told me was vodka.

A MOMENT OF TRIBUTE

Hey, ever notice how
women used to fall
like small republics
on the movie screens
of America? We'd have
the sobbing heroine
fleeing through swamps
or jungles, a parking lot,
or the zoo at midnight
with a spy, husband,
werewolf, man in black,
or free-lance nutcake
in competent pursuit;
and always, the poor dope
would take a tumble

over a box hedge,
or hit a gopher hole
and pull up lame
so those bad hombres
could snatch her up.
Even when the ground
was flatter than
Paul Newman's abdomen,
Miss Ineptitude would
still go sprawling
ass over acting lessons,
and even Snow White
in the big cartoon
had to meet with every
anthropomorphic root

in the enchanted forest.
For our relief we owe
the trimmest thanks to
actress Raquel Welch,
(a.k.a. "Rocky") who
pioneered the art of

staying on one's feet.
I can assure you, after
hours of late night
research, that this
female piston galloped
through movie after
movie without tripping
once, and on occasion
she also turned round

and kicked her pursuer
in the stomach, or
whatever the censors
would permit; and now
we have women all over
dropping gangsters
and lighting zombies.
So pause, escapees,
briefly on your feet for
our forerunner Raquel,
who dodged the KGB,
bulls, dogs, pterodactyls,
and enormous corpuscles;
whose spirits, breasts,
and hemline never fell.

BREAKFAST INCLUDED

Old towns are business: the light
gets reinvigorated, spritzed with sugar
for that syrupy, translucent glister;
you walk through grapefruit cordial.
Libraries: white and filled with diaries.
The food is adorable.
                        Flat stones
in the churchyards have noble inscriptions
and extra room on top, perfect for
nostalgic canoodling. From one till four
there's a woman in a nightgown
sitting on her tomb, telling you
she's her great-great-great-grandmother
who was fatally burned, March 21,
1870, by the explosion
of a lamp filled with R.E. Danforth's
Non-Explosive Burning Fluid.
Her son is playing her son.
Everybody cries, and you mean it.

The Old Plantation Cottage
rents you nightshirts, nightcaps
and warming pans. You're innocent
in that wide, short bed, imagining
a different storm outside
with significant rain, and even if
the night is a total wilt of gentians,
you'll still have muffins
and chocolate hot in the silver.

In exhausted countries,
there's a feeling that love and houses
can grow too old—too wall-thick
and bloody obdurate to let you go.
Not here, not yet. Visitors head home
with pralines; fruitcake; sepia postcards.
Renovated smiles. Bottles of air.

SUNGLASSES, 1970;   THE REST, 1987

Once I went to bed with a boy
just to get his sunglasses off him.
I mean, he never took them off,
never. His roommate Byron
said he wore them in the shower.
So I wanted to see his eyes,
which is a reason,
and I went to bed with him.
Not that I shouted, "This is
all a plot, Johnny Posey,
to get your sunglasses off!"
but I did keep my eyes open
and he did *not* remove the shades.
It was a one time experience.
I had to wait till he was
lying there somewhat dilapidated
and then I snatched them away.
He had nice eyes, actually:
pale blue, indigo rings, and with
crinkles in the corners. They
were very intelligent eyes,
which you might not have thought.
In fact, I'd say his eyes
were the best thing about him,
which might explain why he was
keeping them out of sight.
You shouldn't be listening
for any resonance in this:
it's not about Lonely in America,
it's about fooling around.
For a while it was possible
to bed somebody just to get his
sunglasses off. It was fun
and you got to see people's eyes.
Nobody had to worry about
getting pregnant or sick or
anything. You could go ahead.

All that's going to change now.

WEIRD DOCTORS

There was a dried-fruit
Bertrand Russell type
who tapped my chest
(I was wheezing like a musket)
and told me this
wouldn't have happened
if I'd kept my armpits covered.
Also that chiropractor
who saw the Virgin,
and he wasn't even a Catholic,
although his receptionist was.
And the major loon
who kept on bellowing,
"Cockroaches! Cockroaches!"
and pounding walls and countertops
while his nurse
stared at the ceiling
and I clutched my sheet,
thinking I did not need this
in a gynecologist.

But mostly they're nice enough.
Just weird. Like Dr. Moody
who kept making ladders
with her fingertips
until she finally asked,
"You ever notice
we have just enough blood?
Skin, too. I mean,
a quarter inch less
and we'd all be oozing."
And like my dentist
who glued teeth in bullfrogs
(the dead varnished kind
who play the mandolin
and wear little sombreros).

Though sometimes you never know
what weird is. Or who.

Anyway, they all look like
ghosts, and they all have
quiet thermometers.
My own cousin Lionel
seemed weird enough—
and his white coat weirder—
when he stood looking at
what I'd done to myself
and shouted, "My god, woman!
What have you done to yourself?"
I didn't know.
Aren't they supposed to know?

KNEES AND NECKS / NEW ORLEANS

I was getting my shoulder
jerked back in place when
DeLancie brought Dr. Jess
that nice new book on Medjugorge.
He isn't going again,
not while they're making Yugoslavia
back into Bosnia
and Serbia and Montenegro
and Croatia and Slovenia.
If you look up now,
you don't see the Virgin,
you see a helicopter.

He's going to Guadalupe.
And Dr. Jess said,
"DeLancie, I'm begging you,
don't go down to Guadalupe
and mortify your knees.
Look at Miss Mae Marie's cousin—
six months of agony
with a nephew on either side
hauling her up and down until
I got those two knees fixed,
and, first thing, what does she do?
Takes herself to Guadalupe
and sees those brown old Indians
crawling around the pavement,
and down she crashes in this
fit of Mexican religion.
I told her, 'I certainly hope
you got what you prayed for,'
and she said, 'Dr. Jess,
I hurt so bad I
forgot about praying.'
DeLancie, I saw those kneecaps,
and they were blue and purple

like one of those dab painters
had gotten cute on them."

Despite this flawless expostulation,
I could tell, just standing there,
two fat little candles
had lit themselves
behind DeLancie's eyeballs,
and he had every intention
of packing himself some khaki shorts
and heading on down to Mexico
to fling out both his kneecaps
for a little ecstasy.

Even if you don't go thump
in front of revelation,
embarrassing your friends and
frightening the chiropractors,
the older you get,
it looks like you're going to have
a lot of those little
calcium epiphanies
in the third and fifth lumbars
or maybe the seventh cervical.
The Big O, roller coasters,
or some idiotic football team
scoring a touchdown—
what's the point
if you can't fling back your
head and howl?

That happened to you yet?

PRETTY WOMAN

This lady gets around. Top billing
with stars on the sacred Orpheum,
plus the sun does tricks. You'd better
be Catholic. No Buddhist in Rangoon
ever got one glimmer. Come Christmastime,
we Baptists saw the manger type:
blue robe, chipped plaster nose.
We called her *Mary* in Texas.

In eighteen forty-something,
she was talking a blue Virgin streak,
telling two adolescents
the potatoes would rot,
and babies would die, and walnuts
wouldn't be worth a damn. Sure enough,
potatoes rotted, babies got cholera,
and there was not a walnut to be had
if you wanted a walnut. After that
it was shockers like, *Russia's naughty*.

It's girls seeing girls.
Something happens and wants a shape.
Did you think it was only you
starving to see yourself?
Aquero, "that one," "that thing,"
was the un-French bit of patois
Bernadette called the ghost,
the sedition, that verso of Bernadette:
short, fourteen, acerbic,
nothing like sappy Jennifer Jones
or Darnell dolled up in the grotto.

The rosary's frou-frou, the pouty stars
cosmetic but unavoidable, her feet
maybe not there. What womb, if any,
is under the layers of glow-cloth,
Mary's, or the apple witch's cauldron,
that empty manger? Of those who saw,
how many ever had children?

Bernadette, dowser par excellence,
knelt at the magic mirror
while a candle flickered her fingers.
She never said *Mary*, never went paddling
in her wet, famous stagnancy,
explaining, No thanks, she'd rather
get thermal treatments.

Sorry, I'm just a sucker for this.
It's better than going to the movies
and watching Julia Roberts play a hooker
who marries her filthy rich john.
I hear some girls have seen that thing
thirty times or more.

THE BAD SOUTHERN COOKING POEM

Where I was raised, salt is an exotic spice.
— George Cleveland

I learned to cook bad because that's the way he liked it.
— A wife on television

We cook it like he wants it.
He wants it like she fixed it—
Mama, who was not much
but who sat peeling things
when he was four and empty.
Mama back to Mama
to the first hot Mama
who ever scorched a cow,
because what's love but
Mama and her meat
and the pie with flies?

And the man who
caught the cow says,
"I love good plain cooking."
Meaning his own good Mama:
good woman cooking bad
in his unspiced memory.
Mama shoveling grub, saying,
"Eat it, it's good for you,"
and, by butterbeans, it's not,
though boiled to hush up
small bugs in the collards
and absolutely expurgated
of pimento.

He is eating hot
because we are not trashy;
six vegetables and cake
because somebody might stop by;
six used-to-be vegetables
he doesn't even like

reduced to butterflood and sludge
and salt—the resurrection.

And the man who bought the bacon
hates that simmering green
but he wants it there
like Mama's massacres,
because what's love but Mama
and her heat in heat
and all that tongue sweat?
And the man with the mouth says,
"I love good plain cooking
if you give it plenty of salt."

Daddy back to Daddy back to
umpteenth old Daddy,
laid back in their chairs
dreaming jubilations
of okra and blackeyed pea,
forgetting all that boil
and the turnips with syrup,
and cauliflower redeemed
of any fatal crisp.
They poke the pink
with their Sunday forks and
holler, "Hey, Evangeline,
this cow's not dead yet!"
Mama, they always whisper.
And Mama, still cooking,

comes in to dish the salt:
"Eat it! I'm good for you!"

A GIRL WHO LOVES HER FATHER

Another age, she'd have known
the finicky art of cigar snipping,
staying briefly after dinner
to light the seven stogies
of the men she called Uncle,
moving like a princess
with her classy taper
while the tariff was harangued.
She herself resembles a taper,
pale and long. They call her—
what else?—Princess.

The political now:
she sits in a cautious skirt,
heel nudging instep
at 45 degrees, while papa
speaks directly to the camera.
Her job is to murmur.
It cost big money
to teach her how to murmur.
When he made some birds extinct
and screwed up the Budget
she didn't notice, actually.
She was busy collecting frames
for the shortsighted poor.
She murmurs, "Oh, Daddy!"—
nothing more—
when the jig is up.

Snap her up, young man,
if you plan on travelling.
She will pay, pack and follow
with the best—thin in advance
and proud in beige and pearls.
Trust her to dodge reporters,
paparazzi, men in garages.
Her hair is done.
It will stay done.

Oh, buy her a trim white car!
for she will love you
before God, before the Eagle,
love you like the only other man,
which you now are.
It's blood. It's natural fiber.
Her thin and filial skin.
Which transfers.
Like a decal of our flag.

DOG SUICIDE

My part, I swear, was involuntary.
I was going dead drag slow, planning to park
in the next block at Nancy's, and anyway
I saw that low mob of strays
fibrillating at the curb, getting ready
to do something uncooperative.
But how could I guess this particular
grunge with legs would force himself,
like a wedge, under my right front wheel?

And I, kneeling there on the asphalt,
for one anthropomorphic second truly believed,
He wanted this. Then I thought, *You lunatic,
dogs are NOW! Dogs don't think it over!*

Down at Nancy's, they were eating cheese,
drinking white wine, and asking,
"Where are Martha and Joni?" and we were
with this dog. He was up on his feet,
stunned—so I could sort of touch him—
and smelling the way he smelled
before the car. From what I've learned
reading Dear Abby, a lot of men
would like to stink that way
and can't quite get away with it.

And Joni—next to me all this time—
was sobbing how absolutely awful I must feel.
Truth is: I was only furious.
Mad at a suicidal dog; madder at Joni
for trying to get all over me
with the patented gummy bear hug
she puts on people; furious at the ASPCA
for closing at five o'clock, assuming
nobody ever whacks a dog at night,
leaving me to pound their padlocked gate
like Carry Nation at a forewarned saloon.

Joni started yelling I was insensitive.

The damnedest people call us insensitive,
usually after guzzling our Scotch.
People like Joni, whom I know
loathed my easier time.
She wanted me there, crying.
She wanted to grab that crying,
certain if I wept for a battered dog
I'd weep for her and her worse childhood—
worse than everyone's, to hear her tell it
again and again. Demanding from everybody
what was always too late.

People like my grandmother—
who found me, fourteen, reading
The Feminine Mystique, with my bare feet
propped against her old pump organ—
who hollered, "KIT-ten, why can't you
be SWEET?" Meaning, *You stubborn bitch!*
Meaning, *Why can't I GET you?*
And believe me, you would not enjoy
getting yourself GOT by Eva Hale McFerren,
the granny who told my mother,
"I didn't raise him to lose him,"
and fought poor Mama five years for Daddy.

It begins so easily, you shed a tear
when Tom loses Mary on television,
and you are in for it; the gummy bears
are over you, sobbing, *Oh, baby darling*,
insisting you love in droves,
wanting you SWEET. That being a metaphor
for dumb as the dog, the dog I HAD,
until, finally, this troubleshooter
from the ASPCA came with a noose and
told us to clear off. The dog was snarling,
swiveling on the hip that worked, as if
he had a mind and changed it.

Meanwhile, a dozen real people

waited a block away with finger food,
people to whom I did not have to say,
You can't have what I feel. As for the dog,
I couldn't cry. I haven't. And I won't.

A METAPHOR CROSSES THE ROAD

Sometimes super cool
is nothing more than
pure preparedness.
Like my friend Janet
who was terrified
someday she'd swerve
to miss a dog
and demolish her car
and kill herself
and maybe her children.
For years, whenever
she got behind a wheel
she was thinking,
Hit the dog, hit the dog,
and finally one night
the dog got there
and she slammed
flat across him.

I cried real tears
when Lassie came home,
but I'm worth something, too.
Let's both watch out, dog.

COOL PLACES

I don't like safaris, do not want
anything with coconuts. I pick the
high-up stubborn places:
sunshine like Iceland and comforts
like Nova Scotia. Not that I'm happy
when I arrive. Those normally there
I make as miserable as myself,
grousing about my Southern blood,
demanding blankets. I stare at clots
of spiders, white as Christmas flowers
over door jambs, and get shivery.

So why go? *Easy, a few might say.*
She's hot where she lives,
slogging in the fronds. She wants
a change.

                 No change. My pale family
keeps cool at home. Keeps cool anywhere.
We've forgotten nothing: not a fight,
not a dime, not one contemptuous shrug
at our talk.   We've lived cold-blooded,
craving the welter, the low sky;
screaming our songs with impassive faces,
driving old blades. We've burned houses
with our families inside, then
walked back in ourselves, thin-lipped
at the completeness of it.   Thin lips
built our smiles, thin love our marriages
which endured through glaciers.
We've become soul-scoured, hunkering
on panoramic grudges, and take our cures
in a soul-scouring wind.

                   You want it
for this hatred, like a white fire.

I've been south enough to know
if you've got to choose between
cold quiet hatred and the hot loud kind,
I'd rather take it cold.

WHEN I GET THERE

I was coming downstairs
in my new suede slingback pumps
looking for something
I could cling to, when
I saw two men in khakis
hotfooting it out the door
with the solid oak railing.
And what they'd left was
this stainless steel thing
with a knob at each end
looking for all the world
like a long antiseptic baton
for surgeons who want to twirl.

I'd really looked forward to
that banister with its
smooth-grained irrelevance,
but it seems the good stuff
is always gone when I arrive.
At Kay's party, they ate
all the caviar and cream cheese
while I was parking my car;
the county bulldozed my
picturesque family graveyard;
and, Tommy, you've been
married three years.

EXAMPLES

They locked us up together,
me and these kids, and told me
make them creative
with their pinstripe pads
and oversharpened Ticonderogas.

"Who cares you're only nine?
Can't you remember?"
I put chalk to the board:
*A green swing. Red dirt.
Oil wells. Biting an orange
with a cut on my lip.
Tall, skinny Janis Gandy
lifting me up for a parade.
Me confused with words,
believing Janis was a goose.*
I don't say I'm maybe
the only little kid
ever stomped by a clown.
*Standing by my lamppost
and looking up at the moon.
Trying to paint a cat,
getting two fingers clawed.*
"Is it true?" asks a boy,
thinking what's written
is the opposite of true,
not what's thicker than true.

What's true in particular
is the moon. Not trying to make
a black cat blacker, or a clown
with a bad day, but that moon
between episodes and how I keep
writing it, at fifteen,
at eighteen, and so on up.
Remembering that moon, making it
a trip by itself. Thinking
for the first time, *Let me out.*

ABOUT THE AUTHOR

Martha McFerren received a BS and MLS from North Texas State University and an MFA from Warren Wilson College. She has published three books of poetry, *Delusions of a Popular Mind* (New Orleans Poetry Journal Press), *Get Me Out of Here!* ((Wampeter Press), and *Contours for Ritual* (Louisiana State University Press). Her poems have appeared in *Georgia Review, Shenandoah, Southern Review, New Laurel Review, Stone Country, Plainsong,* and others. She was awarded an Artist Fellowship in Literature by the Louisiana State Arts Council in 1983, a Yaddo Fellowship in 1985, and a National Endowment for the Arts Creative Writing Fellowship in 1991. She lives in New Orleans and is married to one of her better delusions.